D1402274

SIMPLE DEVICES

THE
INCLINED PLANE

Patricia Armentrout

The Rourke Press, Inc.
Vero Beach, Florida 32964

Patricia Armentrout specializes in nonfiction writing and has had several
book series published for primary schools. She resides in Cincinnati with
her husband and two children.

PHOTO CREDITS:
© Armentrout: pages 6, 10, 18; © East Coast Studios: page 13;
© W. Hammer: Cover; © Robin Schwartz/Intl Stock: page 4; © Mike
Lichter/Intl Stock: page 7; © George Ancona/Intl Stock: page 9; © Miwaka
Ikeda/Intl Stock: page 12; © Michael Philip Manheim/Intl Stock: page 15;
© Peter Langone/Intl Stock: page 16; © Christopher Morris/Intl Stock:
page 19; © Michele & Tom Grimm/Intl Stock: page 21; © John Michael/Intl
Stock: page 22

EDITORIAL SERVICES:
Penworthy Learning Systems

Library of Congress Cataloging-in-Publication Data

Armentrout, Patricia, 1960-
   The inclined plane / Patricia Armentrout.
     p. cm. — (Simple Devices)
   Includes index
   Summary: Text and pictures introduce the inclined plane, a simple device
consisting of a slanted surface or ramp to make work easier.
   ISBN 1-57103-176-6
   1. Simple Devices—Juvenile literature. 2. Inclined planes—
Juvenile literature. [1. Inclined planes.]
I. Title II. Series: Armentrout, Patricia, 1960- Simple Devices.
TJ147.A76 1997
621.8'11—dc21   97–15150
                                                                 CIP
                                                                 AC

Printed in the USA

TABLE OF CONTENTS

DEVICES

Devices (deh VYS ez) make it possible for people to do more work with less effort. You probably use many different devices every day without even thinking about it.

There are two types of devices: simple devices and **complex** (KAHM pleks) devices. Simple devices have very few parts.

Some complex devices are made up of hundreds of parts. In fact, most complex devices are really just two or more simple devices working together.

When you ride your bike down a hill you are using an inclined plane.

SIMPLE DEVICES

Simple devices were the first devices to be invented. The same simple devices are still used by people today.

Sloped rooftops allow rainwater to run off.

A playground slide is an inclined plane.

Can you imagine life without the wheel? Some jobs would be much harder without the lever or pulley or wedge. The screw, another simple device, is used in more ways than you might think.

In this book you will learn about one more simple device—the **inclined plane** (IN klynd PLAYN).

THE INCLINED PLANE

An inclined plane is a slanted surface or ramp. You can't get much simpler than that. An inclined plane is a device because it makes work easier.

Have you ever seen furniture movers load or unload a truck? They use a ramp to move heavy furniture from the ground into the truck. The ramp allows the movers to push the furniture slowly up or down. Without the ramp, the movers would have to lift the furniture into the truck.

A ramp makes it easier to load this truck.

GRAVITY

Have you ever taken a fast sled ride down a snow-covered hill? If so, then you have used an inclined plane.

The next time you ride your sled, think about the force at work. **Gravity** (GRAV eh tee) is the force that pulls you down the hill. Gravity is the force that holds and pulls all objects to Earth. Without gravity, inclined planes would not help us.

Combine a slanted surface and slippery snow and you've got a whole lot of fun.

INCLINED PLANES AT WORK

Construction crews use inclined planes. They build roads around mountains. If they didn't, the roads would go straight up and over, which would be too steep for cars and trucks to drive on.

Roads are built around mountains rather than straight up and over them.

Dirt flows easily down the chute of a dump truck.

Work trucks make use of inclined planes. A dump truck couldn't dump its load without the inclined plane! Cement trucks use inclined planes too. They have a chute on the rear of the truck. Wet cement slowly pours from the chute to the work area below.

INCLINED PLANES AT PLAY

Playgrounds have inclined planes. Do you have a slide at your school or local park? You guessed it—a slide is an inclined plane.

Without the inclined plane, there would be no such thing as downhill snow skiing. Put on a pair of skis and aim them down hill. You will soon find how useful—and scary—an inclined plane can be.

Some water skiers use a different kind of inclined plane—a ski ramp. Experienced water skiers, pulled behind motor boats, use large ramps to jump long distances.

Ski slopes are a natural inclined plane.

WATER AND INCLINED PLANES

An inclined plane allows water to flow downward. That is why rooftops on many buildings are made into inclined planes. The sloped roof allows rainwater and snow to slide off easily.

Hot summer days often draw people to cool water. Where can you go for a thrill ride and cool off at the same time? At amusement parks inclined planes and water are used to make water slides and log flumes that are hard to resist.

Water slides are hard to resist on a hot summer day.

INCLINED PLANES IN UNUSUAL PLACES

When you walk up or down stairs, you are walking on an inclined plane. A staircase is one of the most often-used inclined planes.

Bathtubs make use of the inclined plane. They have a very slight slant towards the drain to force the water in that direction.

Stairs may be the most commonly used inclined plane.

Skateboarders perform tricks on sloped walls.

Remember, just about any slanted surface is an inclined plane. How many inclined planes can you find in unusual places?

SIMPLE DEVICES WORKING TOGETHER

Inclined planes are simple, but they are very useful devices. An inclined plane working with other simple devices can create many great devices.

Put an inclined plane with a lever and you can make a seesaw. Put the wheel with an inclined plane and you have a wheelbarrow.

Put many inclined planes with wheels, levers, wedges, pulleys, and screws, and you could build a roller coaster! The most complex devices in the world start with six simple devices.

It takes a lot of simple devices to make a complex roller coaster.

GLOSSARY

complex (KAHM pleks) — made up of many parts or elements

device (deh VYS) — an object, such as a lever, pulley, or inclined plane, used to do one or more simple tasks

gravity (GRAV eh tee) — the force that pulls objects to Earth

inclined plane (IN klynd PLAYN) — a sloped or slanted surface like a hill or ramp

Ramps make it easier for some people to get around.

INDEX